sprouting

Allie Encarnaciòn

BookLeaf Publishing

Presentation by *BookLeaf Publishing*

Web: www.bookleafpub.com

E-mail: info@bookleafpub.com

ISBN: 9789357441339

First edition 2023

dedication

this book is dedicated to my future self.

for everything i'm working towards and everything i know i'll be.

acknowledgement

Thank you to my mom, for loving and leading me endlessly. I don't know how you deal with me (or Leah or David). You are my light, my humor, and somehow you push me forward when I think there's nowhere else to go. I am forever indebted to you.

Thank you Sean. None of this would've been possible without you, not the writing or the growth or the loving or the strength. Your wisdom drives me each day. I don't think you know the impact you have on me and my daily life. I absolutely adore you.

Thank you to my father. Thank you for all the life lessons you've taught me. I interact with them each day, and I'll never forget them.

Thank you to Langston, for dating my maturity, morals, and growth. Just being around you makes my heart fill with love, joy, inspiration, and genuine understanding wrapped in one. Your impact on me has been monumental, even in the short time I've known you. Most of all, thank you for being my equal. I love you, alien. I can't wait to see where we go next.

Thank you to Juan, for embarking on a journey of innocence and emotional maturity before we really knew anything about ourselves. I have you to thank for unconditionality and the strength of the relationships I have now.

Thank you to nature, your miracles and balance. I'm inspired and comforted by you every day.

I know you're thinking I forgot you. But I didn't! Thank you to Valerie, Gabby, Jack, and Adaora for keeping me doubled over with laughter and surrounded by love. I lean on you guys more than you know, and you mean the world and more to me. Thank you to Julia, for keeping me grounded in my values and allowing me to be her best friend in all my years of development. Thank you to Chantal. Pretty girl, you are everything a friend needs and more. I love you so so much. Thank you to Dorothy, for revising this book and reminding me of my power, as a poet and a person. You guys are my chosen family.

if your eyes are the windows to the soul
perhaps the rest of our bodies are the homes
paused the video
started playing the video
our bones are the walls
and brains are attics
memories rusting away fondly like old chairs

my walls are frail
i wish they weren't

as long as your body protects your soul it is the
worthiest thing on this earth

i like that you like it
my body and home

there are people who'd say darker complexions
are uglier
but how melanin is soaked in
adored by the sun
afro sprouting like tulips and garden

your body is your first forever home

started playing the video at 17:50
jumped to 17:31
started playing the video

the welcome mat is our arms, our hands
because of the handshakes we greet people with
and the hugs we tell them to stay with

how do you invite them in though
how do you make it past the greeting and into
something deeper

how do we invite people into our soul
our soul is the only home we have
the only thing that stays after we die

i am very happy to know your soul
to be held in your heart by your home
this is what i mean when i say you feel like
home

i'm falling hard right now
every part of your home is perfect

started watching next episode

started playing the video

i love you

started watching next episode
i love you more

-teleparty chat // home in a soul

taking pure
soft sand
clenching the grains
of the barn's floor
stone and jagged shells
slipping through fingers
cutting soft skin

no tears could fall
god's miracles
are seen in glassy
red-tinged eyes
dry marbles
like glass that cuts palms

an angel
assuaging fingertips
clenching grains
of the barn's floor
making glass
from shared heat
eyelashes to bring
water from marbles
and protect him

-barn floor and glass angel

i hate you so much
that my tongue forgets its second and third
languages
when it hears you speak them

so much that i am not able to go
five minutes without
imagining you at my side

so much that when you hold my hand
or pull me in
sparks run up my spine
and my stomach flutters

so much that i'm sad because you are
and when my emotions flood
past my eyes or curl in my fists
i breathe again because of you

and i am counting down the days
until i can see you again
and buying you gifts
and writing you poems

all because i hate you

-when you ask if i hate you

you'll never get to witness the miracle
of the golden goose falling
on the other side of the street
she will see you.
she will admire your triumphs still.

that trusting golden goose
she loves you still. she
fantasizes your kinship
at every moment.

listen as she sheds her feathers
watch him watch her body.
swim, goose, touch the dark of this water.
never near the sand again.

gold flakes flutter from her skin.
her feet have slowed propelling.
her bill has lost its vanity,
her eyes have welled.

you do not play with the children on the beach,
and when they leave you stomp their sandcastles.
you, you can rescue the golden goose. won't you please?
she is longing for you, again.

you, you wade into the water.
how does the water feel against your hem?
she put them there. she hates you.
still, tell her
does the water tickle your neck, the way it tickles hers?

close your eyes to the navy, lapping against your skin.
make the golden goose jealous, frantic.
when you feel lightheaded, submerge yourself further.
let her flakes cascade around you, ignore her frenzied thrash.

for you to kill the golden goose,
to strip her of her glitters and gold,
you end your own.
only your plight could ruin the golden goose.

please, before you go,
listen to the golden goose
she'll make you a golden raft
golden blanket, golden crown.
she'll weigh herself down with golden brick
to know you have not gone.
yet you are gone.

golden goose, fly far from here.
swim in lakes absent of bodies,
hollow corpses of love.
let the sun form new glitters on your skin.
she will witness the miracle
of the golden goose flying.

-goldwing // golden goose

you want to be everything but friends
you want me to hold you
the way i did.
you want me to hurt you
the way i did.
you want me to kiss you
lay with you
the way i did.

i don't want you to hold me
the way you did.
i don't want you to hurt me
the way you did.
i don't want you to kiss me
glide with me
the way you did.
i want to be nothing

but friends.

-all or nothing

untangling
you. zipping away your skin and prodding
between your organs. placing your
intestines on a glass slide, magnifying
childhood. miss to mrs. i'd make
tables from the distance between your toes
graphs from the slope of your breasts
equations from your black and blues
i'd smother the first flames.

deciphering
you. understand your inner workings;
inner mind. because i am not me without you,
i must know why your mouth
ignites fires. i must understand
why you let him slip gasoline
between kisses. each dollar an extinguisher.
when we were fighting fire the nitrogen
escaped. the fire roared and the nitrogen escaped.
he let out all the nitrogen when we were fighting fire and
the nitrogen escaped

killing you. sirens came and took away your
gasoline man. why did you cry when the fire waned
and stream prevailed, when extinguishers lie in wait of the trash
truck?
i dreamt of killing the gasoline man. i dreamt of killing you. why.
why
did you subject the extinguisher to flame and gas?
no. why did you let your littles see?
i extinguish. mine, yours: the littles do not extinguish.
they are forevermore
deciphering.

appreciating
you. melting to your waves, fusing heat with you.
i cannot be without your fire. you are still on fire. why
are you still on fire? my babies-
i refuse nitrogen. i will not need nitrogen. when all the nitrogen goes
i will take the hydrant. my babies-
they will have the hydrant, the nitrogen. no use
for them. i will never be the flame, never have a gasoline man
my man will kiss with caramel and rosewater and my babies
will never be left
untangling.

does it not scare you?

that you are the fear in my eyes
when you can raise your own hand to become
a monster

does it not scare you?

our tears have cried and dried
your children recoil at your voice
and your palms have become weaponry

does it not scare you?

look at what you've become
the destruction you created
hardly able to pick up a phone though
it's quite easy for you to pick up a belt

what happens when the monster emerges
and catches its own reflection in the mirror?
does he recoil in fear, find kin
equally as terrified, filling with shame and
self-hatred?

or does he ball his fist, filled with newfound power,
exercise control, and
persecute according to emotion?

the monster in the closet
the danger to be protected from
look at what you did to your family
look at what you're capable of.
baby girls in those happy memories
now tainted by the image of your blackout fist
as if the blood and trauma were not
enough of monstrosities

where did you get the edge in your voice from
it was my mother's gift to me
and the emotion? the sadness
an inheritance from my father
do you have anything of your own, then
i would like to think so. i believe my knowledge, my opinions, my love. i believe those are all solely mine
your love? a person?
rather, the way i love. how i adore and how i adore being loved
and the drinks, darling? where did you pull these from?
that is from the sadness
so your father
well. the other boys, too. the loneliness.
are you lonely or are you alone?
i am so very lonely. i am so very alone.

-birthday benefaction, pt. 2 // march 2022

my toes will become tectonic plates
and i am sure i will crumble before you
my nose, eyes; molasses, tsunami

-si te veo de nuevo // 3/23/2022

this is the beginning of the end
the unread emails pile into the thousands
my duvet crinkles atop my mattress
i settle into it at odd hours during the day
soothing heartache and bruises with smothering
pillows
the meds don't seem to be working these days
my head always seems to be aching these days
nothing looks appetizing these days
i never do find the answer to that last problem and
assignments slip through the lines of my agenda
my grades denoted by red marks
i turn off my wifi and pretend the creases in
my mother's brow and concern in my teacher's voice
aren't there. i skip therapy again
(it's been a month now)
and my friends seem to be on another planet
although i can hear their knocks across the wood of
my locked door.
i swim through sleepy oceans of tears. jesus
flooded my path along the seabed,
so godless i am.
my shades are kissing the windowsill
i am kissing death.
it tastes sweet now, littered
across my floor among unclasped bras and seething
sadness.

the end is here. i am kissing death
farewell.

-entering heaven

last summer i turned beautiful
i know because my inboxes overflowed
horny banalities from men
disregarding the fact
i was still underage
i am still underage

it was the summer the
man in the white van trope came true
greasy white man
wiggling a finger as a beckon and a danger
abruptly awakened to kaur's cantaloupe
ms. ratajkowski posing nude

but i was never naked
and the more they grew comfortable staring the
more uncomfortable i got i grew
up into my jeans and my hips rounded out
and all of a sudden i sucked in, stood straighter,
arched more
whenever i sensed an ounce of testosterone around.

and they were always around
commenting on how i posed in the mirror
alone in my room. i was confident they could still see me
and even in that loneliness, i could not escape them
so i embraced them

i embraced them when their compliments
came wrapped in diminishing tones and
disrespect
i embraced them when their eyebrows rose at
my correct calculations, relishing in the fact that i
have proved them wrong
but never questioning why they thought i would be
i embraced them when their calls
from their best friend's corolla
scared me absolutely shitless and yet filled
me with pride at my beauty and my body

last summer, i learned of men and myself
last summer i got a new appeal and a little power
i still don't know how to wield
last summer i was always walking fast
and keeping my head on 360.
last summer, i realized beauty
is in the eye of the straight white cis hetero man,
these notions of beauty as inescapable as the corolla
last summer i learned more about the world
than i had in my first eight years of education
last summer, i turned beautiful

-last summer

tell me everything that's wrong with me
spell it out. young, undeserving girl
rip me apart and count my flaws

when you're done, shower me with love
kiss me into perfection, your little darling
to tremble beneath your affection
then straighten my back again

-angles

my love is so beautiful
marble eyes marble bowl
spilling over. i scoop the ocean in buckets.
my love is more beautiful like this.

grins for gunshots, smiles for stabs
just wait 'till she sees who's under the mask.
a hell is heaven with you
i torture you take i torture you take
an ugly gremlin's dream, a loyal loving subject

i am a sinner
who's probably going to sin again.
my god, you are so beautiful.
when your head is down that way
close your eyes, an abyss. awoken, underwater.

letting the piranhas surround you
just to save you once again
they'll have all but your heart
my love, that is mine to destroy.
i destroy to make, i destroy to make.

make empty promises, love of condition.
condition you must be or else
condition you want to be or else
my love is so beautiful
conditioned. au natural is but a scam,
i want her au moi. i want her pour moi. i want her
chez moi.

she needs to be my desire, she needs to desire me.
delicately
persuade me. tug at my shirt, my smile. harsh, of
force.
my love is so beautiful
rocks are hard places, hard meals. close your eyes,
swallow.
pillow princess prime primal.
my love is so beautiful

if i were a liar
i'd tell her i love her eyes
the curve of her hip
and that her smile brings a glint to her left eye
i'd tell her i love the goosebumps on
the back of her thighs
the hairs on her toes amuse me
and the soft slope of her breast is a comfort
i'd tell her i think it's sexy how her
legs flatten into her seat
i'd tell her i don't mind the freckles on her butt
and remind her that it's okay to
wear tank tops because her
arms really aren't that fat

i'd wrap her waist in my arms
whisper that i love it even when it
can't be discerned from her torso
i'd massage the hump of her shoulder
convince her that broad is a compliment
and enlighten her that everyone has armpit fat
and those childhood scars on her shins
just announce that she's lived
i'd say
you're beautiful and smart
undeniably sexy and crafted by
a being with care and adoration
and i love you for everything you consider a flaw
i love you i love you i love you

-if i were a liar

stuck at sea with those raging waves
sirens call to seduce your body, swim your head
signal your lighthouses, fortify the sail posts

you will not drown tonight.

do you think the bears
ponder their bouncing stomachs
or just eat
and the bees
do you think they check how much pollen
the other bees hold
before they take in any at all?
the birds
babies cooing in their nests
feel no guilt for what they've devoured
take flight

mother nature's children
vessels for self-sustainment,
bodies to experience, not to identify
be like the bears and the bees and the birds
earth's creation and true loves

-the birds, the bears, the bees

the uncertainty in the way
our fingers graze one another
before we finally clasp hands

my voice inaudible
when i need to ask the honest question
afraid of the honest answer
and the dishonest one, too

i don't know if i
will ever feel love
without also feeling doubt

-doubt and love, cousins

running towards
no from
no because
no hatred
running to

and i ran
he was running too
we were running to

for my heart beating my bones
for my legs need to go
for nature and her beauties
for my prospects and my dead ones

running towards

-coleman's sprint

mountainous arms
& a torso of uranium
mossy, rooted, etched legs
hands of stones, mines
his lips like embers

when he smiles
i swear the sun peeks from behind a cloud
when he hardens
another cliff is formed somewhere

& even the gods love him
apollo took special care on his voice
dashing hints of england into american tonation
blessed with never-ending fight by mars
hestia showed him to give endlessly and always

the pull of the moon
on the tides
(i am the tide)
or a warm wind
on a maturing tree
(i am the tree too)

nature gifted me
the love of the earth
soaking me in
its browning gaze. kiss
mint leaves & star fields

a natural love // quad field -

when i grew i grew
a paper unfolding past your box
same time our white car unfolded
across the asphalt's dancing chalk
leaving streaked red metal red
so we warn a green tulip
barely budding baby
of the end of it all
but i just started just
pushing as a new mother
the consequence of man, and in her newness
nights lengthening to behold nothing known
kind high of the induced kind
white car fornicating a black compound
secrets circulating as if you didn't zip my sweaters
kiss tips, torn tights
take new life from life took
colorized future spread upon this road
jiggy this street, discoteca the turns
learn merits, beliefs, love

-past the past

the ends of the universe have been dipped with
my toes. the
urge to slip all the way in has overcome me
more than once
but i cannot be engulfed
i listen to the ville and snoh alegra
sonder, take me with you
there are kisses across my stomach
i have not seen the version of myself that god
has not touched
is it pathetic to cling to
euphoria for one night
and less hours
tamarind, red nail

- *bamboo universe*

www.ingramcontent.com/pod-product-compliance
Lightning Source LLC
Chambersburg PA
CBHW051749130826
49812CB00033B/1070
* 9 7 8 9 3 5 7 4 4 1 3 3 9 *